FAIRY HOUSE
৶ HANDBOOK ৶

FAIRY HOUSE
❧ HANDBOOK ❧

LIZA GARDNER WALSH

Down East

Photographic credits:

Benjamin Magro, front cover and pgs 8, 38

Lynda Chilton, back cover

Amy Wilton, pgs 2–3, 6, 17, 26–27, 30–35, 37, 43, 47, 54–56, 67

Bresson Thomas, pg 5

Liza Gardner Walsh, pgs 10, 12–16, 18, 20–25, 28, 30–32, 34, 36, 40–46, 50–53, 59, 61, 63, 65, 66, 68, 70–75, 77

Brian Jeffery Beggerly, pg 29

Eric Hill, pg 33

Antoine Letarte, pg 39

Ari Meil, pg 48

Emily Lilienthal, pg 49

Nancy Quinn-Simon, pg 52

Michael Maggs, pg 62

Specimen box (pg 40) built by Celeste Crowley

"April Victoria's Lavender Faerie Cookies" (pg 62) originally appeared in the *Herb Companion,* April/May 1993. Reprinted with permission.

Design by Lynda Chilton

BOOKS·MAGAZINE·ONLINE
www.downeast.com

ISBN 978-1-60893-173-6

Printed in China

5   4   3   2   1

Distributed to the trade by National Book Network

Library of Congress Cataloging-in-Publication information available upon request.

To Phoebe and Daphne —
My real-life fairies who make
me believe in magic every day.

❧ CONTENTS ❧

And as the seasons come and go, here's something you might like to know.

There are fairies everywhere: under bushes, in the air, playing games just like you play, singing through their busy day.

So listen, touch, and look around — in the air and on the ground.

And if you watch all nature's things, you might just see a fairy's wings.

—AUTHOR UNKNOWN

Beginning

Step outside. Listen carefully. Do you hear the rustling of wings? The jingle of bells? Do you see a faint orb of light out of the corner of your eye? It may be that there are fairies nearby. Are butterflies following you? Sometimes fairies like to disguise themselves as butterflies. As you walk, look down at the ground for a fairy ring. What are fairy rings, you ask? Don't worry, we'll cover all of this.

If you are committed to taking care of fairies and creating places for them to visit, they are no doubt watching you. And maybe, just maybe, you will catch a glimpse of one of them. Remember, though, that they are very private, and not everyone has the ability to see them. To increase your chances of seeing a fairy, they say you can make a special lotion out of four-leaf clovers or you can look through a self-bored stone, one that has a hole in it made by wind or waves.

Lewis Carroll, the author of *Alice in Wonderland,* offered the following advice on how to see a fairy:

"The first rule is, that it must be a very hot day — that we may consider settled: and you must be just a little sleepy — but not too sleepy to keep your eyes open, mind. Well, and you ought to feel a little — what one may call "fairyish" — the Scottish call it "eerie," and perhaps that's a prettier word; if you don't know what it means, I'm afraid I can hardly explain it; you must wait until you meet a Fairy, and then you'll know.

And the last rule is, that crickets should not be chirping . . .

So, if all things happen together, you have a good chance of seeing a Fairy . . ."

Working with fairies is a trusting business. You build, they come, and every now and again they may leave you little signs that they appreciate your hard work. We will talk about the signs of fairy visitations later, because right now I want to remind you that trying to see fairies is not the only reason to build fairy houses. What are the other reasons, you ask? One is that if you take care of the fairies, they will take care of you. By building them a house, you are appealing to the organized and neat side of a fairy. Fairies love order. The sight of four walls, a roof, and a cleared out space in the messy, unkempt woods gives fairies an infinite amount of joy. Similar to how your mom feels when you clean your room without her even asking (a great thing to try, by the way). But there are more reasons. When one of our young local experts, was asked this question, she said the following about the business of fairy house building. "That's a good question. Believing in fairies is one reason. It can kind of make fairies think humans aren't so bad and maybe then they will show themselves. It also can help you on how well you can build a shelter." Another friend said he makes fairy houses so the fairies "don't feel left out." And one more said, "I feel like I'm helping tired fairies make a pit stop."

Now we need to back up and ask a few vital questions. What is a fairy house? As one of my young friends said very concisely, "it is a small house we build in nature for the fairies." Exactly. But how do you make one? What materials do you use? Are there any rules? Where do you make them? This book

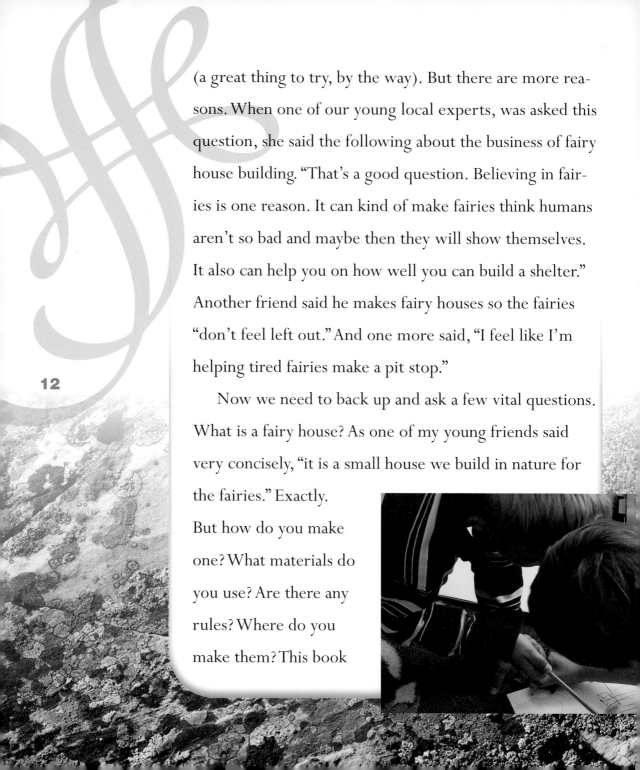

will answer all of these questions. And don't worry, you do not need to live near the woods to build fairy houses. Backyards, city parks, or even a little garden plot will work just fine. Fairies can be comfortable in most places as long as there is green space and natural materials around. Which brings us to our first rule, the biggest, most important, and maybe the only firm rule in fairy house building: fairy houses must be made from materials found in nature.

You got that? Sure, fairies love glittering gems and shiny marbles, but not in their houses! They like admiring these things in the human world, but bring them into the fairy realm and you are guaranteed to make a fairy mad. And a mad fairy is not a good fairy. Don't worry, this is not a problem. The list of materials to build with is long because there are endless supplies of natural materials to choose from.

So, now that we have that covered, here are the most important things that you need as you begin your career as a fairy house builder: a good imagination, an ability to work in the woods for long periods of time, a bag or box to hold the things you collect, a pair of binoculars in case you see something hovering around you while you work, respect for fairies and the natural world, and a good dose of curiosity and inventiveness.

This book is for those of you who have always wanted to make a fairy house but have never dared. It is for those of you who have been making them for years but might need a few new tricks. It is for moms, dads, grandmas and grandpas, aunts and uncles, and anyone who likes to build, create, and be outside. It is filled with pictures of fairy houses made by kids like you. I think you will find as

HOW TO MAKE A
FAIRY HOUSE SCRAPBOOK

If you are making multiple fairy houses every year, then they should be documented. Scrapbooking is a great way to preserve your fairy house building memories and makes a great gift for your grandparents, to boot!

Many stores carry blank books with pretty covers for scrapbooking. Find one that appeals to you and then get ready to create. Gather materials for your fairy scrapbook such as flower and fairy stickers, handmade and decorative paper, glitter and sequins, gardening or nature magazines, ribbons, and buttons.

You will need printed photographs of your fairy house, as well as written descriptions of where your house is located, what materials you used for it, and when you built it. Also, add pictures of you next to your fairy house.

One thing to do when you are building a fairy house is to take a few of the flowers that you used and bring them home to press for later use in your scrapbook. When the flowers are dry and flat, you can add them to your scrapbook.

Find a place to spread out all of your scrapbooking materials and get out your glue and scissors and then have fun creating your scrapbook!

15

you create these little houses that something takes over, that the fairies lead you to the perfect spot to build and provide you with just the right materials, and that the quiet of the woods, park, or your backyard allows your true creativity to unfold. ✧

. . . every child can remember laying his head in the grass, staring into the infinitesimal forest and seeing it grow populous with fairy armies. . .

—ROBERT LOUIS STEVENSON

Scouting

Before you do anything, you need to find a place for your fairy house. A site. And just as if you were scouting the perfect place for a fort in the woods, there are certain things to consider. First of all, given the elusive nature of fairies, does it make sense to put a house for them in the middle of your yard? No! Fairies need plenty of privacy and protection from wind, dogs, and big feet.

As you begin to scout for a perfect site, certain features will attract you — trust your intuition. (You know, that little voice inside of you that tells you not to draw on the couch with magic marker.) Lots of kids are drawn immediately to a certain tree hollow or a space in a

stone wall. The beauty of a fairy house site is that, unlike if you were building a human house, the ground does not need to be level. In fact, your house does not even need to be on the ground. Uprooted trees with their airy roots make amazing fairy houses. One friend made an entire fairy house playground in the roots of an upended tree.

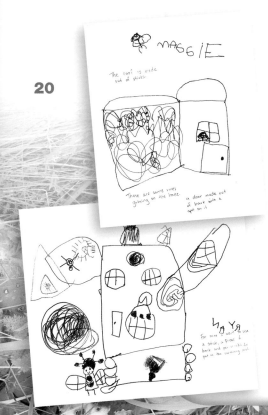

Sometimes, most of the time, the site will dictate what you gather and how you build. But some fairy house builders like to have a plan, even a drawing. If this is how you work, you might want a flat space underneath a big pine tree or a spot in a meadow beneath the tall grass so that your house isn't changed by the landscape requirements. Sometimes drawing a picture of a fairy house prior to

building one gets you in the spirit. While
you draw, consider how you might want
the entrance to look or what shape you
might want the house to be.

If you are building fairy houses with
friends or in a group setting, try to give
each other room. Fairies love a village

and they love to visit each other's houses. So should you. You can gather many ideas from each other. Fair-

ies are not territorial and you should not be, either. You can gather many ideas from your fellow builders and plan together. Fairy villages need more than just a smattering of isolated houses. So work together with your friends to come up with other types of buildings that might benefit a fairy. For example, one group of kids was working on a village and one child found an ear of Indian corn. Well, this find prompted her to create a food pantry for the fairy village. She figured that a town would need a food pantry, and after she had shucked all of the corn

and passed the kernels out to her friends, she said, "I finally got all the corn kernels, now the food pantry is going to get some really good donations."

There are a few special fairy villages where you can visit and add to the collection of fairy houses. In Maine, there is Monhegan Island's famous Cathedral Woods, the birthplace of the fairy house phenomenon. The Coastal Maine Botanical Gardens in Boothbay and Mackworth Island in Falmouth both have well-established fairy house villages. When you go to places like these, it is vital that you use only what is there. Do not bring any of your treasures from home. When so many people come and add things to a natural area, the balance can change. On Monhegan, an island ten miles out to sea, they have a very delicate ecosystem. A few years ago, a local woman collected all of the manmade materials people brought into Cathedral Woods. She found so many foreign objects that she made a boulder-size pile at the start of the trail.

If you are going to build your fairy house on your own, then finding the perfect spot is about following your feelings, picking some place special, or just finding a spot that is close to your house and easy to get to. You might have a special retreat in the woods near your house that would be made even more special with a fairy house. Or you may have a huge willow tree that creates a room underneath its weeping branches. Or a flat rock where you sit after school and read. Just as there are a million ways to make a fairy house, there are endless possibilities as to where to put your house.

HOW TO MAKE A
FAIRY PLAYGROUND

Fairies love to play, so why not build them a playground? Swings, a see-saw, a slide, a sandbox, and monkey bars are all easy to build with natural materials.

Swings can be made in a variety of ways. You can find a rectangular piece of bark and loop two pieces of twine around each side. Attach your swing to a frame made out of twigs. You could also use a piece of sea glass or a flat rock for the seat of your swing.

A see-saw can be made by balancing a piece of bark on a rock.

Sometimes, a slide already exists in nature. Look for smooth rocks that are at an angle or the base of a tree that has lost its bark. Otherwise, find a smooth piece of bark or a narrow, flat rock and lean it at an angle to create a slide. You can build a ladder for fairies to climb or assume they might fly up to the top of your slide!

Monkey bars can be made just as you would make a ladder by gluing rungs to two equal-size twigs. Then make the supporting bars and stand them in the ground.

If you have a sandbox or live close to a beach, borrow a cupful of sand and use twigs to outline a box shape. Acorn caps are good pails for fairy sand castle building.

Here are some of the places where you might want to build a fairy house. You can add to this list as you imagine your own backyard or neighborhood.

Tree hollows

Tree roots and uprooted trees

Stone walls

Beaches

Stumps

Deserted animal holes

Flower gardens

Meadows

Can you think of some other places? You can use the page at the end of this book to make your own list. ❦

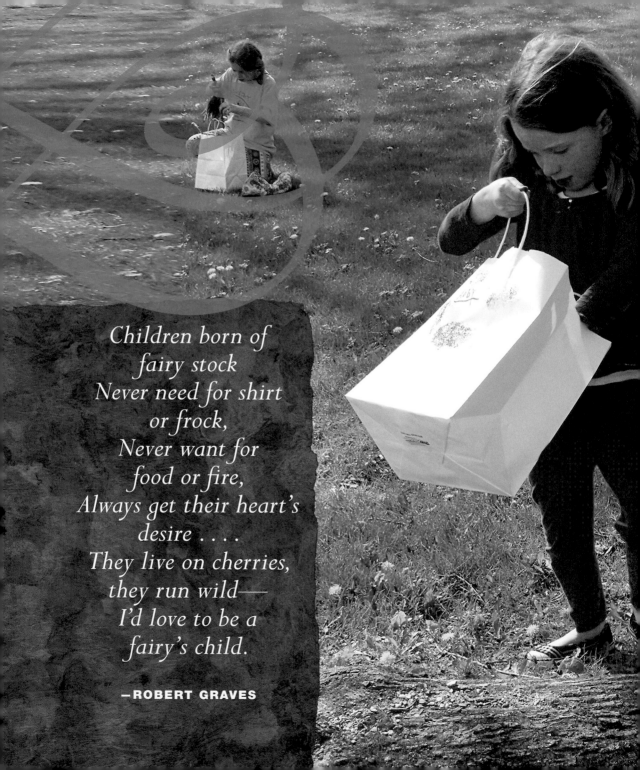

Children born of
fairy stock
Never need for shirt
or frock,
Never want for
food or fire,
Always get their heart's
desire . . . .
They live on cherries,
they run wild—
I'd love to be a
fairy's child.

—ROBERT GRAVES

Gathering

Some of you out there were probably born to collect. When you take a walk, you might stumble upon a bottle cap for your bottle cap collection. Or a button for your button collection. Maybe even an odd-shaped rock for your rock collection. If you have already developed this propensity for gathering, you are in luck. Your well-trained collector's eye will know instinctively what to pick up for your fairy house.

If you are more of a speedy child, getting from point A to point B by skipping, galloping, or sprint-ing, now is the time to cultivate slowness. There are treasures just waiting for you and as you slow down they will emerge. A feather from a turkey or crow. A rock shaped like a heart. A piece of bright blue sea glass. Begin gathering these finds and your fairy house will benefit.

It is these treasures that will make your fairy house comfortable and beautiful to a prospective fairy resident. Twigs, rocks, and bark are the mortar of your fairy house, but sea shells, sea glass, feathers, and abandoned bird's nests are the jewels. Some fairy house builders designate a special bag or box for their collections. Others line the surfaces of their room with treasures. Either strategy works, but on the day of fairy house construction, you will need a sturdy bag or basket to gather even more materials.

Before you venture out, it is a good idea to revisit some of the rules we talked about in the Introduction. I promise that when I say rules, these are fairy rules, not rules like at school. But fairies do have certain standards and so does nature. Those of you who have been at this for a while will recognize some of the rules about fairy house building from this conversation between students at Peopleplace Cooperative Preschool in Camden, Maine. They were asked, what are the rules of the forest when building fairy houses? And they answered as follows:

Eliza: *You can't use squirrels or chipmunks.*

Ryan: *Don't put real glass.*

Delfina: *Don't put dog bones.*

Me: *What can you use?*

Eliza: *You can use fallen-off leaves and sticks that are fallen off branches.*

Mazy: *Don't use rotten bark!*

Eliza: *Yeah, because it won't look pretty.*

Mazy: *You can use bark that has fallen off the tree.*

Maggie: *If you take bark from a tree, the tree will die.*

Jameson: *You can't use stuff from your house.*

Jack: *Or living things.*

Lochlan: *Don't pull up living things 'cause they are nature.*

Lea: *Don't step on the fairy houses!*

Evan: *You can use sticks.*

Jack: *Sticks that are on the ground.*

Lea: *Twigs, berries, rocks.*

Jameson: *Twigs and leaves.*

Lochlan: *Living creatures — don't pick them because they are nature for us to look at.*

Although these kids really covered the bases, here are just a few more rules for gathering:

Do not pull up moss from the ground. Moss takes many years to grow. For example, pincushion moss can take up to forty years to regenerate if it is disturbed.

Do not pick flowers from a garden that is not yours unless you have permission. Fairies absolutely adore flowers. With permission, this is an example of a living thing that is okay to pick for your house.

If you are in a national or state park or at a state beach it is against the law to remove any natural thing.

Be careful of poison ivy. In the summer it is much harder to see than when it turns red in the fall.

And one more thing, if you are outside, certain insects might find you inviting. Always check yourself for ticks after your time in the woods. No one likes ticks, not even fairies.

Here is a list of some things to collect. The list is long, but still does not capture all of the possibilities of materials that are available. Make your own list, add to it constantly.

Shells,

flouawras.

fethars.

Beatees,

stics

Rocks

Poosee WiLLos,

BORck.

Laeus.

wotta,

piNe coNse

Roots.

Leevs.

PoLiN.

hay.

MICA: Fairies are famous for being vain, meaning they really like to look at themselves. Fairies use mica as a mirror to see themselves, therefore, they love it!

POPPY PETALS: Fairies use poppy petals to make clothes. That is why these petals are often called fairy shawls.

MOSS: Okay, one more time — only if it is already separated from the ground.

PINECONES: Little ones, big ones, they all come in handy.

BARK: Birch bark is especially useful in fairy houses as it usually has a nice, curly, silvery quality to it. Other types of bark are great for structural elements of your house.

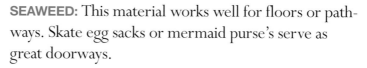

SEAWEED: This material works well for floors or pathways. Skate egg sacks or mermaid purse's serve as great doorways.

STICKS: You can never have too many of these. They are the real foundation for your fairy house.

FEATHERS: Fairies love feathers and they have many uses in your house to soften things up. They are also great for decoration on the outside of your house.

SEA GLASS: Here is your natural sparkle. Sea glass, although not originally from nature, has been tumbled by waves, making it naturally weathered. It is wonderful for decorative accents and windowpanes.

SHELLS: Another essential ingredient for furnishing your house. Shells make great bathtubs and chairs, and small shells like periwinkles make great borders.

ROCKS: Like sticks and bark, stones are vital to your fairy house. They can be used for walls, floors, pathways, tables, and much more.

ACORN CAPS: When acorns begin to fall from oak trees in the fall, you would be wise to start a collection. There are so many uses for acorns, but my favorite is using the tops for bowls and plates.

CAT TAILS: Cat tails usually grow in swampy areas, so be careful when gathering them. You want to harvest them in the late fall when they are dried and ready to die off for winter.

ROSE HIPS: Ripened rose hips can be hollowed out to make bowls and tea pots. You can bend a thin stick and make it into a handle. Rose hips, with their ruby red color, are also lovely as decoration to bring some color to your fairy house.

EGG SHELLS: You can crush egg shells to make a white floor or pathway, or wash them out and use them for fairy containers.

ABANDONED BIRD'S NESTS: They must be abandoned!!! If you are lucky enough to find one of these treasures, a fairy would love to have it as a bed. Fairies and birds are very close friends. The best time to gather them is in the fall.

BERRIES: Never eat a berry in the woods. You know this, though, I know you do. If you are with an adult and you come across a wild blueberry or raspberry and you need a snack, go ahead, but make sure to bring some for the fairies. They love berries. Berries, like rose hips, add some color to your house.

GRASS: A supply you may overlook, but one that is indispensible for weaving, floors, and camouflaging houses.

POPPY PODS: When the poppy flowers wither, they leave a wonderful pod that has a silvery color and an urn shape. This is a great decorative element.

MILKWEED HUSKS: In the fall, gather these milky, fluffy husks for fairy beds. The whispery insides are called "fairy wishes."

CORN SILK: Fairies love this fiber from the husks of corn on the cob. They weave all kinds of clothes and blankets from this material.

REEDS: Like sticks and bark, you can never have enough of this indispensible building material.

PETALS AND FLOWERS: Petals make wonderful fairy clothes, blankets, and rugs. Flowers do wonders to spruce up a drab fairy house and make it festive.

BEANS AND SEEDS: Fill acorn caps with seeds for a fairy feast. Fairies like sunflower seeds, poppy seeds, and sesame seeds. They like to eat beans, but beans can also be used to line pathways and borders.

PUSSY WILLOWS: In the spring, gather pussy willows for fairy pillows.

LAMB'S EAR: The leaves of the lamb's ear plant are like cashmere to a fairy. They are super soft and luxurious and make excellent blankets.

HOSTA LEAVES: These gigantic leaves are great for making roofs, blankets, and bathtubs.

Can you think of any other materials? You can use the page at the end of this book to make your own list. ✾

"Just living is not enough,"
said the butterfly fairy.
"One must have sunshine,
freedom, and a little
flower."

—HANS CHRISTIAN ANDERSEN

Building

So, now you have found a perfect site, planned, and gathered your materials. You are ready to build. The bark you have collected can now be turned into a wall. The giant clam shell can now be turned into a bathtub. Your nook, hollow, or hidey-hole will now become a home for a delighted fairy. You are now an official fairy house construction worker.

Many of you know exactly what to do first. You will build your house with not one ounce of hesitation.

But others might be a bit more hesitant. They might be unsure where to begin or carefully layer twigs across two roots of a giant maple tree only to have them all tumble down. For those

more reluctant builders, remember that a certain amount of frustration is normal in this endeavor. Don't get bogged down. Keep going. Start stacking those twigs again. There are no mistakes in fairy house building, only patience, stick-to-itiveness, and a healthy dose of fairy ingenuity. (Do you know that word? Ingenuity? It is a good word for this hobby, in fact, it sums the whole business up. It means to be inventive or resourceful.) Keep in mind that whatever you do and however you build your house, the fairies will be grateful. As much as I could take this section and tell you exactly how to build a fairy house, there isn't just one way to build a fairy house! They are like snowflakes — never were two fairy houses exactly alike.

The best thing to do is to dive in. Look at your site and your materials and start putting things together. Those twigs and long pieces of grass can be woven together to make a roof. The sheets of birch bark can stand on either side. The perfectly flat rock becomes a patio for the fairies to watch the sunset. What you want to achieve is some house-like form. A-frame or teepee shape. Cabinesque. Hut-like. You want a place where fairies can fly in and rest a while. As one friend said, "I think fairies like medium–size houses because if it is too big they will get lost in it and if it is too small they won't be able to move around too well."

Once you have some walls and a roof, you can begin building the other features: a chimney, windows, and a door. Walkways are fun and since most of you have gathered countless pebbles, seeds, little shells, or small pinecones, you will have plenty of materials for a grand entrance. Think about your own house — the shingles on the roof,

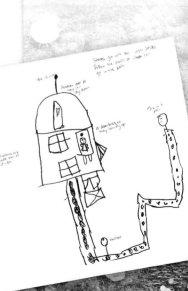

DELFINA

the trim of the windows, the siding. What could you use for shingles — maybe pinecone bracts? (Bracts are a fancy way of saying the leaves on a pine-cone.)

Depending on how big a space you have, your house can have a variety of rooms. A separate kitchen and bedroom. A bathroom. You may ask the perfectly natural question, do fairies use bathrooms? Well, the following conversation came up when some kids were building a fairy house village. My friend Ian said, "I found a perfect toilet seat! It is soft and has a hole in the middle." And then Tatum responded by saying, "I thought fairies went to the bathroom in the woods instead of using the toilet." Hmmm — what do *you* think?

Not every fairy house needs a door and not every way of constructing will allow for one. But say you found a piece of driftwood with a hole worn through the center — well, use it as your door. Another technique

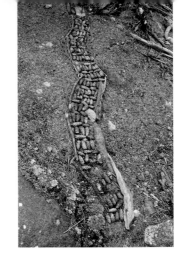

is to find a V-shaped stick and use that to form an archway into your house. Some fairy house builders spend a lot of time constructing their doors. One friend weaves twigs together to make a rectangle and then rests it up against the house. Personally, I think fairies value a little privacy. Being a fairy is hard work and they might just need a nap away from the peering eyes of woodland creatures.

Another aspect to consider is the landscaping around your house. As I said earlier, fairies love order. Clearing out the area around your site promotes this sense of tidiness and makes room for a fairy garden or outdoor dining area. A nicely laid out garden or pathway is as important

as your actual structure.

But let's get back to the construction zone for a second. We have an issue that needs to be addressed — a big debate in the fairy house world. The question

is, to glue or not to glue. Can you use glue when building a fairy house since it is, after all, a man-made material?

I say if you want your fairy house to last, a little glue can't hurt. One fairy house purist I know recently used a sharp rock to puncture a hole in a piece of bark and then took seaweed and tied it through to bend it into a bowl shape. Now that is commitment. This is the same amazing person who said, "I don't think fairies really like glue. When they build their own houses, they must have a way of not using glue." I have heard of fairies using sap to attach things, but I wouldn't recommend this as you will get uncomfortably sticky. I leave the choice to you, however. You can weave a piece of grass around twigs to make ladder rungs or add a drop of glue at each step and move onto another part of your house. One of my favorite uses for glue is in making sea glass windows. Sea glass bordered by tiny

HOW TO MAKE A STAINED GLASS WINDOW

Heat your glue gun and remember to work with an adult when using a hot glue gun.

Select pieces of sea glass that are flat and square.

Find either thin branches or dried reeds to use for the window trim. I like using dried daylily or hosta shoots because they can be cut with scissors.

Make a cross out of two reeds or branches and glue them together in the center of the cross.

Take your first piece of sea glass and put glue on the right angle of the sea glass and then fit it into the cross. Repeat with the other three pieces of sea glass.

Use scissors to trim any of the extra reed or branch that extends past your sea glass.

Now measure the width and length of your window and cut your reeds or branches so that they outline the edges of the window. Depending on the shape of your sea glass, you might need to bend the reed or branch to fit.

Voilà. You have made a window for your fairy house! You can make birch bark shutters by simply cutting two rectangles the same length as your window and gluing them to either side.

twigs looks elegant. Remember the pinecone shingles I mentioned earlier. (The pinecone bracts.) A little glue will go a long way with that endeavor. Again, it is up to you. I see nothing wrong with an occasional dab of glue and I think fairies ultimately will enjoy the elaboration that glue allows.

So step back and look at your fairy house. Pat yourself on the back, for you have taken all of the elements you gathered and created this beautiful and unique dwelling. I can almost hear the fairies clapping. But we are not finished quite yet. It is time to make the fairies comfortable, to "feather the nest," as they say. ❧

46

Faeries, come take me out of this dull world, For I would ride with you upon the wind, Run on the top of the dishevelled tide, And dance upon the mountains like a flame.

—WILLIAM BUTLER YEATS

48

Accessories

Now it's time for the really fun part. Yes, we *have* had fun already. But now the objects you have gathered take on a life of their own. The mussel shell becomes a sling-back chair with a Queen Anne's lace pillow. The flat rock becomes a tabletop set with a rose hip tea set and acorn cap plates.

What does a fairy house truly need for furniture? The size of your house will determine how much furniture you need. Just as we thought about the elements for the outside of your fairy house by imagining your actual house, we can do the same thing with the accessories inside your house. Think of how much stuff is inside your real house: tables,

chairs, a couch, toys, beds, a bathtub, bookshelves. The list goes on and on.

At the very least, you can make a little table with some chairs or a simple bed and a lamp for your fairy house. Lamps can be made from small pinecones or poppy pods set on a stick, or if you are really lucky, a Japanese lantern flower. These globe-like orange flowers look just like a lantern. You can make elaborate headboards for your bed by assembling twigs and decorating them with berries, shells, or seaweed. One friend took a hosta leaf and stuffed it with grass and sewed it with a long piece of straw to make a very comfortable mattress. Put a lamb's ear blanket and a pussy willow pillow on this bed and some blessed fairy will be asleep before they know what hit them. If you happen to have access to rose petals or lavender, your bed will not only be comfortable, the scents of these plants will make the fairy have sweet dreams. If you were fortunate enough to find mica, you now can have a mirror. As I mentioned in the gathering section, fairies love to look at themselves and so this feature will certainly attract them. A rug is a nice addition and as you look at your collection of leaves and petals, one might jump out as a good one for a fairy to walk upon. Rugs woven out of reeds, stems, and grasses, although time-consuming to make, last longer than a leaf or a petal.

The list of accessories and furnishings for your house is as big as your ability to come up with them. You might think of accessories that no one has thought of before, such as one friend who built a fairy telescope. Or one who used a prickly horse chestnut catkin as a protective fairy helmet. Or another who made a fairy scarecrow.

Here are some quotes from kids like you as they transformed their findings into accessories.

"I made a flag with a shell on a stick."

"I found a sunbathing rock."

"I have a great idea—you know that shell, put valuable rocks in it and have it be a treasure chest."

"We found a baby snail; it is going to be a fairy pet."

Another thing to think about in the accessory realm is fairy clothing. Fairies love clothes. There are certain fairies whose only job is to make endless costumes. Try your hand at being a fairy seamstress. There is a woman named Nancy Quinn-Simon who makes amazing fairy clothes out of dried flowers. She presses the blossoms and petals and then, when they have dried, glues them onto paper clothing templates. Some of her designs include a nasturtium gown, a viola jersey, and a pair of thyme shorts. You can try this technique or you can simply take a large petal and cut it with scissors. You can cut a hole in the center of a petal or a leaf to make a fairy poncho. A bigger hole will make

52

HOW TO MAKE A ROSE HIP TEA SET

This activity is dependent on perfectly ripe rose hips from a *Rosa rugosa* bush. Rose hips are a brilliant red when they are ripe and should be slightly soft to the touch, but not too squishy.

Gather them in several sizes. The biggest can be made into a tea pot, medium can be turned into a sugar bowl or a creamer. Smaller rose hips can become tea cups.

Lay out your rose hips on a cutting board and ask a grownup to help you. Use a small knife and gently cut a circle around the top of the rose hip. Be patient, because sometimes the rose hip will collapse.

Once you have cut around the top, you are ready to scoop out the seeds. Wooden coffee stirrers or Popsicle sticks work well for this task.

Now, you are ready to make the handles. Gather some leaves and cut off the stems. Cut off the little bumpy end of the stem. Look at your hollowed out rose hip and bend the stem to see how long you need to make the handle.

Pierce the end of the stem into the lower end of the rose hip, supporting the inside with your finger. Now bend the stem and press into the upper part of the rose hip. This might take a few tries. Again, be patient.

Now you can fill your cups with sweet juice and nectar for the fairies to enjoy!

53

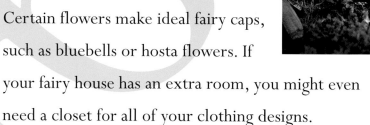

it a fairy skirt. You can even put little berry buttons on your fairy fashions. Certain flowers make ideal fairy caps, such as bluebells or hosta flowers. If your fairy house has an extra room, you might even need a closet for all of your clothing designs.

A word about housekeeping. Don't roll your eyes; we are not talking about cleaning exactly, more like maintenance. If you have made your fairy house in your back yard or somewhere close by, you can continually refresh it. Certain accessories, like the Queen Anne's lace pillow, will not last longer than a few days. This allows you to update your house according to the seasons. Peony petals make beautiful curtains or blankets in early spring, but by October you can use a bright red maple leaf instead. Checking on your fairy house and keeping it fresh and tidy will make it a sure favorite for the fairies. And that is why you did this in the first place, right? So now, how do you get all those fairies to stay for a while? Read on.

The fairy poet takes a sheet
Of moonbeam, silver white;
His ink is dew from daisies sweet,
His pen a point of light.

—JOYCE KILMER

56

Attracting

You have worked hard. Someone who has worked as hard as you should have the opportunity to see a fairy. There are no guarantees, but now that you have built your house, perhaps they will come. You may have friends who have already seen a fairy. Like the little girl who said she "saw a big fairy one time, but there was only one because she was the only one available." Or another, who "was jumping on a trampoline and saw a spot in the forest lighter than the other part, kind of sparkly."

As I said earlier, there *are* ways to try to force the issue. Remember the four-leaf clover and the self-bored rock tricks? Remember Lewis Carroll's words of advice — hot day, a little sleepy, no crickets chirping. They do say the best times of day to see a fairy are just before sunset, twilight, and midnight. Fairies love summer, so they tend to come out in the largest groupings in mid-summer and especially on the summer solstice. In fact, I have heard many times that if you leave a fairy cake (a miniature pancake) in a bed of thyme, the fairies will come that night and eat it up. Here is some more advice on seeing a fairy, which needs a bit of a translation from the Olde English to get the full effect.

"To enable one to see the Fairies: a pint of sallet oyle and put it into a vial glasse; and first wash it with rose-water and marygolde water; the flowers to be gathered towards the east. Wash it till the oyle becomes white, then put it into the glasse, and then put thereto the buds of hollyhock, the flowers of marygolde, the flowers of the toppes of wild thyme, the buds of young hazle, and the thyme must be gathered neare the side of a hill where fairies use to be; and take the grasse of a fairy throne; then all these put into the oyle in the glasse and sette it to dissolve three days in the sunne and then keep it for thy use."

-RECEIPT DATED 1600

If you have successfully trans-
lated this advice, you will note that you
first have to find where the fairies are or
have recently been in order to make the
potion to see fairies. That is a tall order.
If you try these tricks and potions and in
fact see a fairy one day, do not look away.
You will only see the fairy for as long as your eyes stay
focused on it.

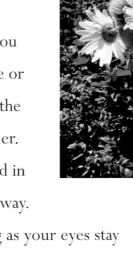

A quick word of precaution. Most fairies are kind
and generous. They love children, especially those who
build them houses and villages. But there are some
fairies whose heads are filled with mischief. To avoid
these troublesome sorts, you merely have to wear a
daisy chain upon your head. You don't *have* to do this
because there is only a very slim chance that mischief
will come to you while building a fairy house. To make a
daisy chain, gather daisies with stems at least five inches
long. Use your fingernail to slice a one-inch slit into one

stem. Insert the stem of another daisy through the slit and pull. Repeat this until you have a complete chain. It should take six or seven daisies. If you are making a fairy house in the fall or early spring and there are no daisies around, not to worry. You can make leaf crowns, black-eyed Susan, or dandelion chains. The important thing is to wear some sort of circular crown on your head. Circles are symbols of magical protection and no fairy would dare to mess with someone wearing one.

With this in mind, the same is true for finding a fairy ring. A fairy ring is a place where fairies meet to dance and sing, usually in the middle of the night. A fairy ring

can be a circle of stones, a ring of toadstools, or a circle of thicker, darker colored grass. Do not disturb a fairy ring whatever you do, for they say the Fairy Queen will immediately take you to Fairy Land and it is much more difficult to get out of Fairy Land than it is to get in. You can make a fairy ring of your own by placing rocks or shells in a circle and perhaps the fairies will have a party there.

But what you really want to know is if the fairies are actually using your house. If they are resting on your beautiful hosta leaf mattress. Or gazing at themselves in your mica mirror. Or perhaps sipping tea out of your acorn cup. Some friends used the following techniques to test whether or not fairies were truly visiting their houses.

"One time, we left bread in our fairy house and the fairies left a marble and a crystal." "One time, I made a book that said *show yourself* on the front. The next day when I came to look at the book, there were scribbles in it."

These are great ideas and there are even more ways to attract fairies to your house. Fairies love when people leave milk in a little shell or hollow so they can give their fairy babies milk baths. They will settle for clean water, but fairies do have a soft spot for milk, cream, and butter. I don't know why. They also love sweet things like fruit, jam, and cakes. That is why it is a good practice to make a tiny pancake for the fairies on those days when your family eats pancakes. We have included a recipe for a nice lavender cookie that fairies simply adore. If you have bluebells growing in your garden, they are a favorite flower food for fairies, and they also use them to make hats.

April Victoria's Lavender Faerie Cookies

- ½ cup butter
- 1 cup sugar
- 2 eggs
- ½ teaspoon vanilla
- 1 ½ cups flour
- 2 teaspoons baking powder

Preheat oven to 375°F. Cream butter and sugar. Beat in eggs and vanilla; stir in the dry ingredients until well blended. Drop by half-teaspoons on ungreased baking sheet. Bake 8 to 10 minutes, and cool slightly on baking sheet before transferring to tiny plates.

HOW TO MAKE A FAIRY FLOWER PERSON

Find a stick that is shaped like the letter Y. Then find another straight stick that is smaller than the first one. The Y stick, when turned upside down, is your fairy flower person's legs and the smaller stick is the arms.

Make a cross with the two sticks with upside down Y on the bottom. Connect the cross with either a dab of glue or wrap a long piece of grass around the intersection to secure. This center point is the body of the person.

Find some kind of round shape to form the head, such as a poppy pod, a bud or the middle of a flower. Stick the top of the Y into this round piece and that is your head.

Next, take any sort of a petal and tie it below the arms of your person with another piece of grass. This is the skirt for your person.

You can add a hat by finding a pointed flower like a blue-bell or a daylily.

Never put iron in a fairy house — it is something fairies just cannot tolerate.

So now you have done your work, kept out the iron, added some bluebells, and generally tidied up the place. If you haven't left a book or a snack, how do you know if a fairy has visited? When you investigate, there are certain clues that will tell you if fairies have been in the area. Note if there are any ripped leaves around your fairy house. Or fairy dust sprinkled on the moss. Fairy dust looks a lot like glitter, but the grains are miniscule. Perhaps there are some holes drilled into a piece of bark near your fairy house, or some strange squiggly lines in the surrounding dirt. If there is a spider's web near your fairy house, check to see if there are pieces of the flower clothing you made resting on top, as fairies dry their clothes on spider webs. If you go out hunting for fairy evidence in the early morning, you might find dew that is tented above the grass. This is called a moisture

HOW TO MAKE A FAIRY BED FRAME

A fairy bed is one of the most essential and fun accessories in a fairy house. This is just one example because there are no limits on how and what you can use to make a fairy bed.

Find a piece of birch bark that is relatively flat. Using scissors, cut a semi-circle out of the bark.

Heat your glue gun and remember to have an adult with you while using one.

Gather berries, small shells, bright flowers, or sea glass, and arrange a design onto the piece of bark.

Use your glue gun to attach your design onto the bark. This is the headboard for your bed.

Now, find a stick that is about as thick as your thumb and break it into three pieces, two long pieces and one the same width as the head board. Using your glue gun, create a frame. Place the two longer pieces on either side of the headboard and the shorter branches on the top and bottom.

Fill the frame with moss, lamb's ear, leaves, or flower petals and your fairies will have a wonderful rest!

canopy. A dew tent is a sign that fairies were having a party and the canopy is a remnant of their big evening.

As you wait for a fairy to grace your house, take stock of your achievements. Whether or not you ever see a fairy, you have shown, as my friend Tatum said, that humans aren't so bad. You have spent time outside working in nature, using your intuition and your ingenuity. (Remember those words?) And from now on, every time you go into the woods, you will know exactly what to do to make a fairy house. There is no limit to how many you can make in a lifetime. There is no age at which you need to stop building. I know people who have been making fairy houses for more than fifty years. Keep working and taking care of the fairies. Continue to listen for the jingle of bells or squint your eyes as the air shimmers around your fairy house. There is magic in building these houses and I hope you always treasure it. ❧

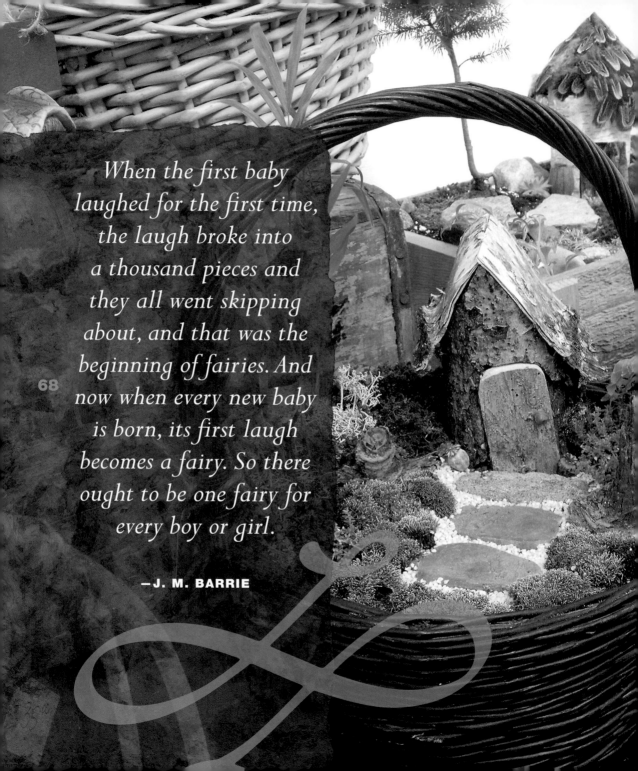

When the first baby laughed for the first time, the laugh broke into a thousand pieces and they all went skipping about, and that was the beginning of fairies. And now when every new baby is born, its first laugh becomes a fairy. So there ought to be one fairy for every boy or girl.

—J. M. BARRIE

Expanding

Portable Fairy Houses

What if you could take your fairy house with you? If you could bring it on vacation to your grandmother's house? Or bring it inside when you felt lonely. Well, then a portable fairy house might be just the thing. A portable fairy house is basically a container garden that is designed with plants and accessories to attract fairies. You can use any kind of container, from a basket to an old window box. Fill the container halfway with dirt and then begin to gather a collection of plants. What makes fairies enjoy these little habitats is the use of herbs and dwarf plants like creeping thyme and dwarf myrtle. You can use other herbs such as

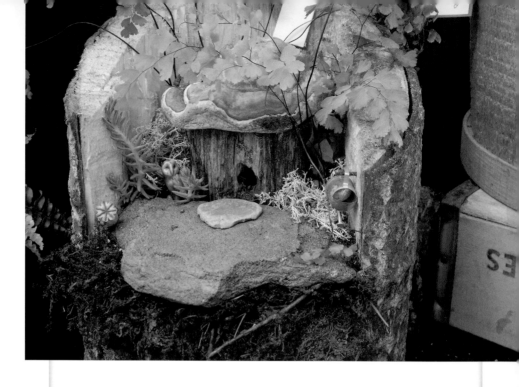

oregano, germander, lavender, and marjoram.

Before you plant anything in your portable fairy house, think back on our fairy house work and make a plan. Between the plants, you can create a pathway for the fairies that ends at a small rock bench. Perhaps you have some extra bark to create a shelter at the center of the container. Since your portable fairy house is not set in nature, you can use man-made materials. Bring on the shiny things. Those lovely glass mosaic pieces can form a little stream. There are amazing fairy garden accessories available, such as miniature watering cans and mailboxes. Kerry Day, who owns Mini Me in Greene, Maine, has a great eye for the details one needs in a portable fairy house.

Once you have completed your portable fairy garden, place it in a sunny spot and give it plenty of water. The landscape will change as the plants grow and you can add and take away accessories as you see fit. When winter comes, bring your little garden inside to a sunny window and who knows, maybe the fairies will follow.

Troll and Goblin Houses:

Say you have read through this entire book and decided you've had enough of this fairy business. You are ready to build a house for someone far more grumpy, messy, and accepting of improper behavior. You may think fairies are all well and good, but I want to see someone

grotesque — like a goblin — or catch a troll in daylight and make him turn into stone. Do you think that is what happened to this fellow in the photo to the left? Maybe you are ready for a little more mischief than a fairy can provide. Well, then this section is for you.

Take off your shoes. Wear something really old that maybe your mom and dad hope they never see again, because goblin and troll houses rely heavily on mud. Yes, mud. Close your eyes and imagine your fairy house. Now imagine the exact opposite. Instead of flowers, gnarled roots form decorative elements. Instead of a

bed of soft grass and pussy willows, picture a bed made out of rough bark or prickly nettles. Now, this is not

LIFE-SIZE FAIRY HOUSES

Once you have mastered making houses for little people, you can use those same skills to make a life-size fairy house for you and your friends.

Follow the same steps used to make a fairy house. Find a site, gather your materials, and build.

You will need to find a site next to a tree or big rock to support your structure.

Gather big branches and sticks as tall as you are, or even taller. Make a big pile of these sticks. When you feel like you have enough to build a good shelter, start building.

Start with one stick and lean it at an angle up against the tree or rock that you are using for support. Repeat this process, laying the sticks next to each other to create a wall. Make sure you can fit beneath the structure you are making before you build too much.

You might want to make a broom out of a branch with leaves to sweep the inside of your fort once it is finished. You can also gather piles of leaves for a bed and find some rocks for stools.

73

to say that making a home for a goblin or a troll doesn't take skill or inventiveness — it just requires a very different set of parameters than fairy house building. Whereas fairies like order, goblins and trolls like chaos. Where fairies truly appreciate costumes and accessories, the only clothes a goblin or troll desires are the ones on their dirt-covered bodies. We can still follow the same formula that we used for fairy houses: finding a site, gathering materials, and building the house.

What constitutes a good site for a troll or goblin house? Many of these creatures prefer dark, cavernous spaces. Dirty. Trolls especially like the dank spaces underneath bridges. But for our purposes, as well as for the goblins and trolls, I recommend the giant mud-coated roots of upended trees. They are gnarled, menacing looking, and provide many areas for house building. If you can't find a big uprooted tree, perhaps a rotted stump would work. You could even dig a hole and cover it with slimy seaweed.

What do you gather for these types of houses? Anything nasty, cracked, or bro-ken. Bring a bucket and fill it with mud. The mud will be like plaster, which you can apply with a pine bough or your hands. While the mud is wet, plan on adding some stones and crushed leaves to make a floor. This is your palette. Add whatever rotting things you can find. Nothing shiny, nothing bright. The key to attracting a goblin or troll is *not* to make your house beautiful or inviting. It is to make it look disgusting but, and here is the art in this endeavor, still a place where a tired goblin or troll might want to rest their head. Do they use pillows? You decide. Tables? Probably not.

The very best thing about making a house for these somewhat unpopular creatures is that they will know you are trying to help them. Imagine how it feels if everyone always made a special place for your cousin but you were completely ignored. Don't you think goblins and trolls might feel a bit left out? By "befriending" — and I say that very loosely as you really don't want these guys as your friends — you are protecting yourself from receiving any of the mischief that a goblin or troll can cast on a human.

After you build your goblin or troll house keep an eye out for footprints. If you see large bugs or harvested mushrooms, you will know one of these creatures has found your house. Try not to linger and bother the troll or goblin. They are not particularly fond of children. But if you do set your eyes on one of these characters, you never know, they might give you a wink for taking care of them. It can't be easy being so disagreeable all of the time, right? And even if your friends haven't quite caught on to building goblin and troll houses, I say give it a few years and there will be troll dens and goblin grottos all over the woods. Just make sure that after a day of this work, you take your shoes off before you go inside. ℘

Recommended Reading & Resources

Further Reading:

The Secret Life of Fairies by Penelope Larkspur

Fairy Houses by Tracy Kane

Fairy Houses… Everywhere! by Barry and Tracy Kane

A Field Guide to Fairies by Susannah Marriott

Fairyopolis: A Flower Fairies Journal by Cicely Mary Barker, Glen Bird, Liz Catchpole

Fairy Houses of the Maine Coast by Maureen Heffernan

Fairy Island: An Enchanted Tour of the Homes of the Little Folk by Laura and Cameron Martin

The Fairies Ring: A Book of Fairy Stories and Poems collected and adapted by Jane Yolen

Articles from the magazine *The Herb Companion*, "Gardening with Fairies," "Where the Wild Thyme Grows," and "What the Fairy Best are Wearing this Season." www.herbcompanion.com

Sources for portable fairy houses and fairy gardens:

Mini Me – Kerry Day, kerryday@fairpoint.net

Market Hill, www.finefairyhouse.com

For invaluable fairy house information:

www.fairyhouse.com, Tracy and Barry Kane's amazing Web site.

And for invaluable information on fairy clothing:
Nancy Quinn-Simon, carlylefarm@aol.com

Here is a list of just some of the many fairy and fairy house festivals throughout the country. Fairy house festivals are sprouting up all over, so check in your community for events or start your own! Botanical gardens often have fairy house workshops, as do libraries and art centers.

Fairy Festivals

May Day Fairy Festival in Glenrock, Pennsylvania, at Spoutwood Farm
Usually held in late April or early May. www.spoutwood.com

Maryland Faerie Festival in Darlington, Maryland
Usually held in May. www.marylandfaeriefestival.org

New York Faerie Festival in Ouaquaga, New York
Usually held at the end of June or early July. www.nyfaeriefest.com

Fairy House Festivals

Maine Fairy House Festival at Coastal Maine Botanical Gardens
in Boothbay, Maine
Usually held in August. www.mainegardens.org/events-and-programs/
special-events/maine-fairy-house-festival

Tour of Fairy Houses in Portsmouth, New Hampshire: World's Largest Fairy
House Event
Usually held in mid-September. www.fairyhouses.com/eventspage

Fairy House Festival at ArtPark in Lewiston, New York
Usually held in June. www.artpark.net/content/pages/family-events-fairy-
house-festival

Fairy House Fantasy Fest at Meerkerk Gardens in Greenbank, Washington
Usually held in July. www.meerkerkgardens.org/calendar.html

Fairy Glossary

Fairies go by a number of different names, and there are many types of creatures who are related to the fairies. Here is a list of just a few of them.

Bogie Beast: A playful and sometimes naughty goblin.

Brownie: A type of hobgoblin that helps with household chores.

Dwarf: Tend to be short, stocky, humanlike, and also very good at mining.

Elf: A small and often mischievous creature from mountainous areas who tends to use magic to interfere in human activity.

Fairy: The term that encompasses the whole race. The word fairy comes from the Latin word *fatae* which means fate.

Frid: Magical creatures who live under rocks and like to be given milk and bread as offerings.

The Gentry: In many cultures, it is not a good idea to say the word fairy as there are so many types and you might call upon the wrong kind. This is a polite way of saying fairies without getting yourself in trouble.

Giants: Monstrously huge beings who resemble humans. They are a type of ogre, but once in a while, giants can be friendly.

Gnomes: Dwarf-like creatures who live underground and guard treasure.

Goblins: Ugly, small, and generally gross creatures who are truly mischievous.

Good People: Another polite term for fairies.

Hobgoblin: A mostly friendly and accommodating spirit who doesn't shy away from occasional mischief.

Lil Fellas: Another polite term for fairies.

Mermaids: Fairies of the sea who are half fish and half woman.

Neckan: A river spirit who plays the harp.

Portunes: Tiny fairies who come to people's fireplaces at night and roast frogs.

Spriggans: Possibly the ghosts of giants who have the ability to turn from very small to huge.

Trolls: A cave-dwelling unattractive creature that can either be the size of a giant or a dwarf. If a troll is caught in daylight, it will turn to stone.

Urisk: A creature related to brownies who is half human and half goat. They are thought to be lucky to have around as they are very helpful with farm work.

Fairy House Form

Date	Location	Materials Used	Photo or Drawing

Date	Location	Materials Used	Photo or Drawing

Date	Location	Materials Used	Photo or Drawing

Acknowledgements

Writing this book was a lot like building a fairy house. Lots of pieces were gathered and many hands were used to put it all together. I am grateful that Tris Coburn scouted for a fairy house writer and that Ari Meil let me be the one to write it. Ari was an encouraging and gentle force throughout this process and is responsible for the inclusion of goblin houses. Thank you also to Michael Steere for seeing the book through to the finish line and for his calm and patient manner.

Thank you to Tracy and Barry Kane for starting the fairy house phenomena and for being so gracious and supportive of this project.

I want to thank Peopleplace Cooperative School for being so open to fairies and fairy house building. If I were a fairy, I can think of nowhere else I would want to visit. Thank you Heather Bowen for all of your pictures, quotes, love of nature and little houses, and to all of the teachers for taking such good care of my family.

I have never been much of a photographer and would have been lost without the supplements from Amy Wilton, Iris Eichenlaub, Emma Peabody, and Kathleen Meil.

The kids who attended the Rockport Library workshops were such a great source of energy, ideas and quotes. Thank you to William Jurek, Annabelle and Abby Williams, Jack Lawrence, Harper Coburn, Julianna Day, Ian and Julian Henderson, Jesse Bifulco, Tatum Dowd, Alexandra Southworth, and Tessa and Calder Meil. Thank you also to Girl Scout Troop 1822 and their fearless leaders for letting me commandeer a meeting. All of the neighborhood kids in the Grove Street Gang contributed in some way to the ideas in this book. Thank you especially to Sunny Conlan, and Ava and Luke Tobias.

Thank you to everyone at Rockport Public Library for making the library a sanctuary to all of us in this community. Thanks especially to Molly Larson and Bob Peabody for the ultimate gift of time to work on this book.

I am not sure how to begin to thank my friends and family. The list is long and my friends and family are near and far. I love you all. My mom started all of this by allowing me to stay home on days when I wasn't even that sick so we could make little mouse houses and work on our dollhouse. Thanks to my dad for always believing in me and telling such good bedtime stories.

Phoebe and Daphne are the true maestros of fairy house building. Thank you for your endless enthusiasm for this project and willingness to stop everything to build a piece of fairy furniture. Thank you Jeff for your continued patience, love, encouragement to grow, and willingness to hold down the fort. I am so lucky. ✤